WHAT IF

A HISTORICAL FICTION NOVEL

BY

CARLOS WALKER

ISBN: 978-0-578-80753-9

Printed by Power of Purpose Publishing
www.PopPublishing.com
Atlanta, Ga. 30326

Acknowledgements

First and foremost, I would like to thank God. For without him, this project would never have come into existence.

Next, I would like to thank my parents Hilton and Inell Walker to whom I place my tenacity in which I strive. My father who passed a few months ago, but whose spirit still pushes me to do better daily. All I can hear is "I Clare Boy," to those who knew him would understand. Then there is the sweet but mean woman I love with all my heart, my mother (My Queen.) She has been the hustler of all hustlers so I try to use her skills to make this work (Ma we still grinding). Even though I am no longer a child, I will always be their child. I will always seek their approval. I find myself looking for my father even though physically he is no longer with us. I just pray that I haven't failed them, and I thank them for never giving up on me, and for always being there.

I want to thank my siblings; Debra, D.D (D'andre), Luvinia, Eric, and Erica. All of whom have supported me while I was locked up creating this masterpiece. I would like for all of you to know that although it was hard, you all made it easier just answering the phone and by coming to visit when you could. You lift my spirit even now that I have been released with words of encouragement. Plus, you all have inspired me to be the best me possible. Especially you Luvinia, and most definitely that crazy ass brother of mine.

Now, to one of my biggest inspirers. The woman whom God placed in my life at a time when no one was there but family and she is one I still hold dear. She has helped me get this project out in many ways and I owe her. Thank you for all you have invested. It's a blessing having you in my life.

I want to thank a few fellas I was locked up with Tosumbi Jones, one of my biggest critics. Also, I don't want to forget Super Bless (Orlando Fuller), Noc, Mr. Hicks, Mr. Sarge, Robert Quintanilla, and Mr. Wali McCullough for their inspirational insight that they shared throughout that process.

I want to thank everyone that I may have missed, know that the love I have for you isn't that I didn't want to shout you out, it's just too many to name. Lastly, thank you Cody for my upbringing because without home I'm nothing.

"Injustice anywhere is a threat to justice everywhere"

~ Martin Luther King Jr.

"I'm for truth, no matter who tells it. I'm for justice, no matter who it is against. I'm a human being first and foremost, & as such I'm for whoever benefits humanity as a whole."

~ Malcom X

The racist mainstream media had failed America, the report concluded: "The press has too long basked in a white world looking out of it, if at all, with white men's eyes and white perspective."

"Our nation is moving towards two societies, one black, one white-separate and unequal."

~ Kerner Commission

"I may not change the world, but I bet I spark the mind that does."

~ Tupac Shukar

Contents

CHAPTER 1

The Introduction of Slavery

In 1619, the first nineteen white slaves were captured in Africa then transported to America. These white Africans were brought to America to become indentured servants. They were bound by this duty against their will. These indentured servants were put under contract for a period of at least seven years. Truthfully, that time frame lasted a lot longer because of the master's inscrutable desire for free labor.

In 1651, many of the first nineteen white indentured servants had fulfilled their obligation. Most of the first nineteen did in fact, gain their status of Freedmen/Women.

In 1680, the institution of American slavery developed and became statutory law. Under this system, a white African slave was chattel; an article of property that could be bought, punished, sold, loaned, used as collateral, or willed to another at an owner's whim.

The white African people were not recognized as people in the eyes of the law.

Thus, they had no legal rights. These people were viewed in the same respect as farm animals. They were to be worked, and they were to be bred. The offspring of the slave belonged to the slave's owner regardless as to whether one of the parents had his/her freedmen status or not. This way, their children would continue to be slaves in their masters' fields until …

The Arrival

Slave ships owned by black Dutchmen and black Portuguese arrived in Jamestown, VA in 1619. Slaves were traded to the black colonist that were in Jamestown for food and other goods. This was the first exchange in recorded history.

Between 1619-1859, eleven million white captives were ferried across the Atlantic North America where their futures were replete with mental, physical, and emotional torture and anguish. For this inhumanity was the hallmark of the forced servitude that these white captives had to endure.

Over the next 240 years, the transatlantic slave trade proved to be a very profitable enterprise for the black British, French, Dutch, Spanish, and Portuguese who carried it out. North America opened a lucrative place to transport and sell white African slaves. Yet, the transatlantic slave trade also reached other countries such as South America, Europe, Middle East, and the Caribbean.

All of which combined for an enormous growth of wealth across the world. Much greater wealth would have been accumulated had not so many white slaves been lost due to cruelty, disease, and suicide.

CHAPTER 2

Whites For Sale

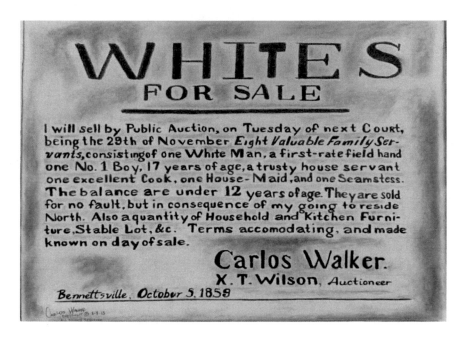

When Carlos Walker, a black slave owner, decided that he wanted to move his family north, he posted a public auction notice. Mr. Walker was putting property that he no longer wanted or needed up for auction. This property consisted of a white slave family of eight, and some household supplies.

The posting of a public auction notice was the procedure used to get the word out when one wanted to sell their slaves.

The Branding

It was a standard operating procedure for the slave to welcome their new merchandise to the plantation by placing a brand somewhere upon the body of the slave.

The branding was a way to distinguish one owner's property from another slave owner's property.

The brands also denoted ownership in the case of run-away slaves. The brands were brutally placed upon the slave's body using a red-hot iron or poker.

The Auction Block

The auction block is where slave masters went to purchase and sell slaves. Slaves were bought to these auctions to work on the master's plantations. Also, every plantation owner kept a keen eye out for slaves that they would purchase for breeding purposes. The slave owners wanted healthy, fertile females and strong studs to breed with the female slaves. If the slaves reproduced regularly, the owner's assets continued to grow, allowing them to increase their slave inventory to work their plantation.

Mr. Walker held his public auction in Bennettsville, S.C. on October 5, 1858. On this day, there were many affluent black slave masters waiting to purchase Mr. Walker's property.

The slave family that was sold were separated from one another. The mother was sold to the McCollough plantation where she would toil in the household. The children were sold to separate slave traders heading to Mississippi and New Orleans, respectively. While the father was sold to the Gibson plantation where he would be used to breed and labor in the tobacco fields.

CHAPTER 3

The Help

Most slaves were given names of their master's choosing. However, the slaves were referred to as "The Help." Yet, more often … derogatory words such as "Cracker," or "Honky" were used to get the attention of the slave when the master or another black citizen needed the slave's services (e.g. "Cracker get over here and fetch me a cold glass of water.")

Although the slaves were provided with names, these derogatory terms were used to degrade the slave and keep the said slave in his/her place.

CHAPTER 4

The Product of Rape

During slavery, many black slave masters used their female slaves for their personal enjoyment. These female slaves were often referred to as bed wenches. It did not matter what the female slave's marital status was. The slave master could take his sexual pleasure anytime it pleased him to do so. This was a form of legalized rape.

Rape was just one of the many ways that a slave master showed his dominance over his property. However, the slave master's sexual interest in his female slaves often subjected that female slave to the abuse directed at her from the master's wife. The master's wife usually directed the anger that she felt because of her husband's dalliances at the female slave who truly had no choice in the matter. The female slave was also often mistreated by other slaves because of the slave master's treatment of her.

The slave master's treatment of their female slaves was really one of the most insidious methods used to destroy the slave's household. The master would seem to be giving the female slave special attention when all the while he was treating her like a piece of trash and degrading her. The master's rape and impregnation of the female slave was also a means of degrading the male slave that she was courting or married to. This created yet another problem for the slave family. The atrocity that had been committed against his women left the male slave often feeling worthless for being unable to protect her from the slave master. The children produced from rape would often be both loved and despised by the mother's husband who would valiantly attempt to love the child as his own. Unfortunately, the effects of these rapes are still evident today.

The Escape

After years of forced labor and all types of inhuman treatment (i.e. beatings, rape, lynching, being bought and sold like livestock, etc.), a great number of slaves reached the limit of their endurance. These slaves sought their freedom by any means possible.

For most, the means that was used was escape. The slave would steal away in the night and attempt to make it up north where there was freedom from slavery.

The Capture

Now, when it was discovered that there was a run-away slave, the black slave master along with other plantation owners would release hunting dogs and hunt the runaway slave like a wild animal. The slave would then be brought back to the plantation for punishment. The punishment was always carried out in front of the other slaves and consisted of a variety of tortures ranging from: whippings, dismemberments, and lynching.

These tactics were used as a means of discouraging any further attempts to escape by other slaves.

CHAPTER 5

The Whipping Post

The whipping post was used as a tool to induce fear as well as to reduce resistance. Whenever a slave master wanted to break the spirit of a slave, remind a slave of his/her rightful place, or for any perceived infraction that was deemed worthy of punishment, the slave was tied to a post. The slave was then beaten mercilessly with a bullwhip which stripped flesh from the slave's body. At times, the slaves were beaten to death.

Scars of a Slave

The white slaves who had attempted to escape or had resisted the complete dominance of the black citizenry were easily distinguished by the horrific scars that they bore on their backs.

The slave masters intended for these scars to serve as a warning to other slaves. However, the scars along with all the other inhumane treatment motivated some slaves to begin to fight back.

The Slave Revolt

After decades of abuse, with no end in sight, some slaves who were fed up with the life they were living decided to fight back. These slaves decided they would rather die fighting for freedom than to continue to suffer at the hands of their black masters.

History was recorded that one of the great slave rebellions was led by a slave who was a preacher named Nat Turner. Turner organized a large group of slaves and revolted.

The revolt resulted in sixty people being killed including slave masters and their families.

After the insurrection, more than 200 slaves were slaughtered. Turner himself eventually got killed. However, his fight for his unalienable right to be free will forever be remembered as spurring the coming of a new era.

PART II
THE COMING OF A NEW ERA
JIM CROW

CHAPTER 6

The Klan

In 1863, after President Abraham Lincoln signed the Emancipation Proclamation, all slaves were officially set free. This act signified the abolishment of the horrific institution of slavery in the United States. It was also the impetus that formed groups of hate mongers that would become known as The Ku Klux Klan.

The initial group of Klansmen was made up of ex-confederate soldiers. These black soldiers felt the loss of the war, their way of life, their property, and their wealth. This fostered a vile hatred that was directed toward former white slaves. This hatred was manifested in various forms of harassment and torture ranging from cross burnings to lynching.

This organized black group of the Ku Klux Klan spread an ideology through the black population stating that these former white slaves were going to become their equals. Or … that the former slaves would become vengeful and turn the tables enslaving those who once enslaved them. The spreading of this ideology ensured that the ranks of the Klan grew.

Naturally, the spreading of this ideology induced fear In the black community. This made it easy for the southern states to pass Jim Crow Laws. The Jim Crow Laws were designed to keep the children of former slaves underfoot for as long as the Jim Crow system stayed in place.

In 1916, the film "Birth of a Nation" was produced. This movie depicted the Ku Klux Klan as saviors. The Klan was to save the Black Americans from the decedents of former slaves.

The Hanging

Between 1882 and 1930, 3,386 thousand whites were lynched by the Klan and other frustrated blacks who bought into the Klan's ideology.

Oftentimes, these lynchings were turned into a celebration. Black folks would gather and have a picnic, drink and toast and take pictures. They would even bring their young children to these atrocious gatherings to ensure that this evil would become a tradition.

Naturally, these inhumane acts were being committed without any form of legal recourse, instilling fear in the white community.

The black Klan used cross burnings and lynchings as their calling card. This madness proliferated across the south and it promulgated the Klan's message of black supremacy.

CHAPTER 7

The Tuskegee Syphilis Experiment

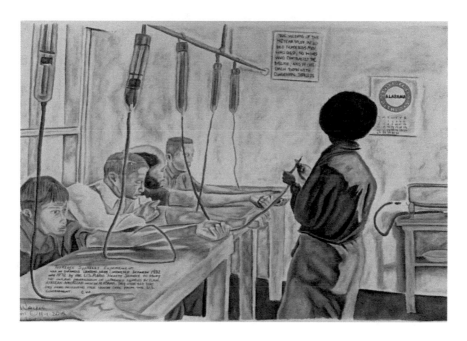

Between 1930 and 1970, the government conducted experiments on the white community. These experiments took place in Tuskegee, Alabama. Under the pretense of free vaccination shots, the government injected white people with the syphilis disease.

During this forty-year span, the government did find a cure for the disease. However, the cure was never administered to any of the test subjects. Instead, the government monitored those individuals like lab rats. In cruel fascination, they watched as the disease progressed and spread to spouses and children.

CHAPTER 8

Rosa Parks' Defiance

In 1955, a portion of the Jim Crow Laws forced the white people to sit in the back of public buses. These same laws also had a provision that allowed a black citizen to appropriate a seat that was occupied by a white person (who was viewed as a second-class citizen) if so desired.

One day, Rosa Parks, exhausted from working all day, decided to take a stand. Ms. Parks chose not to give up her seat when a black man told her to move because he wanted the seat. By refusing to obey, Ms. Parks broke the law and was arrested.

Ms. Parks' arrest led to thirteen months of boycott against the public bus system. The boycott led to all the whites abstaining from using public transportation, this led the busing system to lose a tremendous amount of revenue.

For it was the white people who made up majority of the bus riding population.

1957 Integration of the School System

In the late 1950s, the Federal Government mandated that all public schools be integrated. However, there were states that would not willingly accede to the integration of their public -school system. In fact, some in the South did not do so until the late 1960s.

At schools that had traditionally been all black, the parents, the faculty, and the student body did everything in their power to make the experience of attending class uncomfortable for the white students. The goal was to get white parents, and the white students to choose not to attend black schools.

CHAPTER 9

A Fight for Equal Rights

During the Jim Crow Era, it was common practice for whites to be refused service inside a black-owned restaurant or diner. White folks would have to go to the back door to order and to pick up their food.

At the end of the 1950s and beginning of the '60s the Civil Rights Movement was in full swing. White people started picketing and staging sit-ins inside black-owned establishments. Through the perseverance of these protestors, this practice of inequality came to an end.

Malcolm X: By Any Means Necessary

Malcolm X, born Malcolm Little is known for his religious and political activism and controversial advocacy of white unity. The intensity of his convictions and the eloquence with which he articulated his beliefs are still inspirational to this day.

While serving a ten-year sentence for armed robbery in the state of Massachusetts, Malcolm became a member of an organization called "The Nation of Islam." After Malcolm became a member of the Nation of Islam, he rid himself of the family name that had been handed down to his family from their former slave masters. He was no longer referred to as Malcolm Little, he became known as Malcolm X.

During this time the government and media referred to the Nation of Islam and its members with the derogatory term "White Muslims" to distinguish them as subversive.

Malcolm X advocated white unity and independence. He believed that white people should protect themselves and their rights from the abuse of the black establishment "By Any Means Necessary."

The White Panther Party & The Defiance Against Injustice

Huey P. Newton and Bobby Seal, two white men, founded the Panther Party in 1966, in Oakland California.

The Panther Party was an organization whose sole purpose was to help the white community by providing services that went lacking in the community. These services included feeding the children every morning before school, teaching white history, selfdefense tactics, and protecting the white community members from the brutality and havoc the racist black law enforcement routinely dispensed upon the white community. This helped to give the whites a voice in the on-going Civil Rights Movement. However, as the Panther Party grew, so did their opposition. J. Edgar Hoover, director of the F.B.I, at the time targeted the Panther Party. Hoover, a known racist, did not believe that whites should have the same rights and respect as black citizens. Therefore, he made it his mission to destroy, ironically by any means necessary, any group or person that fought for civil rights.

Thus, under the guidance of J. Edgar Hoover, the F.B.I strategized to dismantle and destroy the white Panther Party. This goal was accomplished by several plots ... from infiltrating the organization causing distention amongst the ranks ... the frame-ups of leadership, to lies and propaganda that led to deadly disputes with other white organizations.

Still, the Panther Party will forever be recognized as a pillar of the white community.

The ideals the White Panthers stood for ... their bravery and defiance in the face of overwhelming odd makes the white community thankful for their existence ... because to the Panther Party ... White Lives Matter.

CHAPTER 10

Symbolism: Sayin' Grace in Jesus' Name

One of the insidious methods that blacks used to subjugate the minds of other races was to portray God as being black.

As Christianity spread across the world, early artists inevitably painted Jesus Christ, the Son of God, as a black man. This began the subtle but undeniable brainwashing of all. For if the Son of God is a black man, then God himself, is a black man. Naturally, those of the black race would see themselves as superior to those of other races.

After so many generations of this erroneous belief being instilled in black children, the erroneous belief had become ingrained in those of the black race.

Therefore, it was easy for blacks to decide that they would kidnap, torture, enslave, and strip the native culture from the white Africans for they felt entitled to do so.

After committing these horrendous acts, the blacks then proceeded to teach generations of white Africans that their only hope was in Jesus Christ whom they continued to portray as a black man. This subliminally caused the whites to see themselves as inferior.

The Justice System

The justice system has many components, one of which is the penal system. In theory, the penal system has a twofold purpose: 1) punish those convicted for the crime that was committed, and 2) rehabilitate the convicted criminal.

However, the rehabilitation purpose soon took a back seat to the cheap labor force that the convicted felon provided to the state and/or federal government.

To ensure that this cheap labor force continued to grow, the establishment strategically targeted the white community.

By keeping the masses of white citizens undereducated and introducing various drugs in vast quantities into the white communities, the establishment guaranteed that a high percentage of white citizens lived at or below the poverty level. Thus, a large amount of the white citizenry would see crime as a viable option for survival.

The government then passed numerous laws that would ensure the mass incarceration of white citizens... creating a self-perpetuating cycle.

PART III
A NEW ERA BIRTH OF
WHITE LIVES MATTER ERA

CHAPTER 11

The White Lives Matter Organization

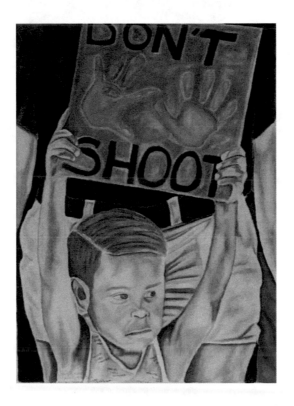

The White Lives Matter Organization was founded by three brilliant women: Alicia Garza, Patricia Collors, and Opal Tometi. They were fed up with the senseless killings of unarmed white men and women. These three women chose to act after the senseless killing of Trayvon Martin by a black neighborhood watchman. Essentially, these women got on social media and started the hashtag #WhiteLivesMatter to give a worldwide voice to the subject. And that voice resounded. White Lives Matter soon became a movement.

White Lives Matter is an organization that stands up for the lives and rights of white people. Why is an organization like this necessary? History has shown that from the time the first white Africans were kidnapped and transported across the Atlantic, their lives and/ or well-being only mattered as much as the monetary profit could be gained by keeping them alive.

Since that time in America, every successive generation of those white African descendants have been subjected to unspeakable horrors and atrocities that testify to the fact that white lives have never mattered in this nation.

The White Lives Matter organization wants to change America's view on how white life is valued. This organization wants white American citizens to be respected as much as black American citizens.

This younger generation of white Americans has picked up the mantle of the civil rights movement.

Unfortunately, the White Lives Matter organization has been labeled a hate group by some black Americans. However, choosing to say, "White Lives Matter," in no way negates the fact that **_all_** Lives Matter. It only shines a spotlight on what has been/is strategically done to the white American people.

The organization has encouraged white African descendants all over the world to stand up for their rights. This movement is not going to end until … White Matters.

CHAPTER 12

I Can't Breathe
(Eric Garner)

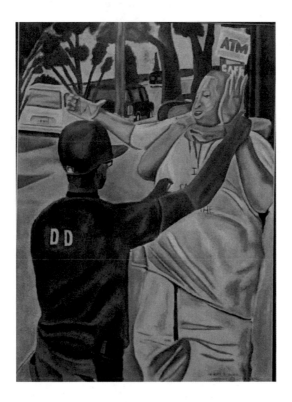

On July 17, 2014, an unarmed New York native, Eric Garner, was murdered by the hands of an NYPD officer.

It is reported that Mr. Garner was selling loose cigarettes when he was approached by NYPD officers. During the confrontation, an officer chose to forego conflict resolution attempts to de-escalate the situation and chose instead to escalate the encounter by applying an ILLEGAL chokehold on Mr. Garner.

As the chokehold was being administered, Mr. Garner, uttered the words, *'I can't breathe.'* This utterance was caught on tape and was heard by the officer that was administering the chokehold as well as the accompanying officers. Still, the officer administering the chokehold did not loosen his grip, nor did any of the other officers do anything to intervene.

Although the video of Mr. Garner's tragic murder was broadcast nationally by news outlets across the country, the officer responsible for taking Mr. Garner's life was later justified and cleared from any wrong-doing.

The Department of Justice's failure to prosecute this officer only emphasized the lack of respect for minorities in this country. Which prompted people to protest in New York City and many other metropolises across the country.

CHAPTER 13

The Murder of Tamir Rice

November 22, 2014, in Cleveland Ohio, twelve year-old Tamir Rice was murdered by a police officer. Why? Because he was a white child playing with a toy gun.

In this nation, young boys have been playing with toy guns longer than anyone can remember (e.g. cowboys and Indians, cops & robbers, military games etc.).

Unfortunately, for Tamir, he was not cognizant of the overall social climate of this nation nor the racial stigma attached to it. That is ... if you're a young white male, you are guilty of some type of criminal behavior automatically.

Therefore, when a "concerned citizen" called 911 and informed the authorities of a "possible" case of a child with a gun, the incompetent dispatcher failed to inform the responding officers that the gun was "possibly" a toy gun. So, within two seconds of these overzealous responding officers pulling up to the scene, shots were fired, and young Tamir had been executed.

Clearly, this is yet another example of the different policing standards for blacks and whites. The investigation following this incident cleared the murder of Tamir Rice as a justifiable homicide. Once again, proving that the authorities don't believe that … White Lives Matter.

CHAPTER 14

The Assassination of Walter Scott

April 4, 2015, A South Carolina native, Walter Scott, was murdered by a police officer in Charleston, SouthCarolina.

Walter Scott was pulled over under the suspicion that he was operating a vehicle without a license and that the vehicle he was operating had illegal tags on it.

Once Mr Scott pulled the vehicle over to the curb, he immediately exited the vehicle and fled. A foot-chase pursued, all of which was recorded on the officer's body camera.

CHAPTER 15

Freddie Grey's Mysterious Death

On April 12, 2015, twenty-five years old, Freddie Grey was brutalized by two Baltimore police officers in Baltimore Maryland.

When Baltimore police officers pulled on to the block where Freddie Grey and his associates were hanging out, the entire group of young men took off running. Of course, the officers gave pursuit. By the end of the chase, Freddie Grey had been brutalized. On a video recording, it appeared that Mr. Grey had suffered some type of spinal injury. The video shows Mr. Grey could not stand up, let alone walk.

Mr. Grey was handcuffed, dragged, and thrown into the back of a police patty wagon.

Mr. Grey was not stabilized by any means in the back of the vehicle.

Therefore, Mr. Grey was left to be bounced and tossed around during the 45 minutes that he was driven around in police custody. This jarring only exacerbated the trauma that Mr. Grey had suffered at the hands of the arresting officers.

Later, Mr. Grey was found dead in police custody.

The six officers involved with the handling of Mr. Grey were charged and acquitted.

No one would be held accountable for Mr. Grey's death. It was that demonstration by the establishment of how little White Lives Matter that ignited a riot in Baltimore.

Baltimore Riot for Freddie Grey

The Baltimore youth, fuming with indignation and absolutely fed up with seeing fatality after fatality at the hands of police officers gave rise. Seeing police officers by and large get away with murder as if they had a license to kill fueled the young community.

These young people decided that they had to act to get the attention of the nation and to show the police what they were feeling inside. They wanted the nation and the police to realize that … White Lives Matter.

CHAPTER 16

McKinney, Texas Police Officer
(Goes Wild at Pool Party)

On June 5, 2015, in McKinney Texas, a group of teens were at a pool party. For some reason, the police were called.

When the patrolmen arrived, one of the officers looked at these white adolescents and became extremely reckless and hostile. When these young people started verbalizing how they felt about the blatant disrespect that this officer was showing them, the officer singled out an adolescent female and very aggressively apprehended her.

A few of the young men, seeing how this officer was manhandling the young female, attempted to get him to stop his abuse. However, the officer, full of rage, pulled his service weapon and began chasing the three young men.

Of course, this horrific incident caused an uproar in the white community. The parents of the young lady, along with most of the other adults in the community, requested that this unprofessional officer be fired for his conduct. Unbelievably, the officer was never charged with any wrongdoing. Instead, the officer was allowed to resign ensuring he could keep his retirement benefits.

Although this case was clearly an unjustifiable assault on a minor, this officer of the law faced no type of punishment. The entire incident just underscores the lack of respect for people of these teen's color.

CHAPTER 17

Charleston Church Massacre

June 17, 2015, in Charleston, SC a massacre took place inside a community church. The then members of Emmanuel African Methodist Episcopal Church were having bible study when Dylan Roof entered the church. Mr. Roof was the only black person in the building. However, he came in pretending that he needed prayer.

Naturally, the good people of the church lovingly embraced him offering him prayer and solace. Suddenly, Mr. Roof pulled a firearm and killed nine people in cold blood.

Mr. Roof's sole intention was to murder white people. This despicable man chose to leave one of the church devotees alive to make sure that someone would be around to tell the story of his brutal acts.

A Heroic Act of Defiance
(Bree Newsome Removes the Confederate Flag)

June 27, 2015; ten days after the massacre at Emmanuel African Methodist Episcopal Church in Charleston, South Carolina, North Carolina native, Bree Newsome along with a group of other protestors assembled in front of the South Carolina State Capitol Building. This group was protesting the fact that the state capitol flew the confederate flag. The confederate flag is the same flag that was embraced by the slaveholding states when they chose to secede from the union. It is also the same flag that has become a symbol of racism and hatred since the slaveholding states lost the civil war. The confederate flag is also the same flag that Dylan Roof pledged his allegiance to prior to his going into the church in Charleston and slaughtered nine innocent people.

It was during this protest when Bree Newsome, as an act of defiance against this hate symbol (confederate flag), decided to climb the flagpole and remove the symbol of hatred.

Ms. Newsome was summarily arrested and charged with "defacing a monument."

However, in the eyes of her people, Ms. Newsome will always be remembered and respected as a young hero. Yet, in the eyes of those blacks who believe in the hatred that the confederate flag represents, Bree Newsome will always be despised.

CHAPTER 18

S.A.E Fraternity Chant

A group of S.A.E fraternity members were caught on video camera spewing this racist chant:

"There will never be a "CRACKER" at S.A.E"

"There will never be a "CRACKER" at S.A.E"

"You can hang him from a tree, but he can never sign with me" "There will never be a "CRACKER" at S.A.E" "There will never be a "CRACKER" at S.A.E"

The video of this chant got public attention and immediately garnered the public outcry of the vulgar rhetoric and blatant racism. To the credit of the University of Oklahoma, all the fraternity members caught on camera were expelled and the chapter of S.A.E fraternity has been suspended from the University.

CHAPTER 19

Texas Teacher Smacks Student

On April 11, 2016, within an elementary school in Texas, a young white boy was brutally attacked by his black female teacher.

The attack was videotaped by another student. The teacher was filmed repeatedly smacking this young child at least five times. The entire time she was subjecting the child to the physical attack, she was also emotionally demoralizing the child with verbal attacks by repeatedly calling the child "stupid."

Naturally, this attack sparked outrage amongst the white community and the teacher was eventually charged and fired for her misconduct.

CHAPTER 20

The Assassination of Alton Sterling

Baton Rouge, Louisiana; Alton Sterling, also known as "CD Man," was going about his daily routine of selling CDs in front of a neighborhood store when he was wrestled to the ground then shot in the back by law enforcement officers.

This incident was precipitated by an anonymous call to the police stating that Mr. Sterling had brandished a pistol at someone. When the black officers approached Mr. Sterling, a white man, they did so in an aggressive and hostile manner. They immediately wrestled Mr. Sterling to the ground, shot him in the back, killing him instantly.

The Murder of Philando Castile

Minneapolis, Minnesota, Philando Castile, a typical working white man was murdered in broad daylight, in front of his fiancé and her daughter by a black patrolman.

Mr. Castile was pulled over in a traffic stop because of a faulty taillight. When asked for his license and registration, Mr. Castile respectfully let the officer know that he had registered a gun in the vehicle and that he was the owner of the gun.

As Mr. Castile reached for his registration card, he was gunned down by the officer.

While all of this was taking place, Mr. Castile's fiancé was streaming the incident on Facebook Live. Amazingly, this young woman kept her composure. While the officer claimed that he had told Mr. Castile not to reach for his registration, this young woman told him and everyone who was to see the incident that he was lying.

After watching her fiancé be killed, this brave young woman had to suffer the indignity of being treated like a criminal. This young woman and her daughter were taken into custody and placed in the back of the police vehicle. It was then that the young lady finally broke down crying.

This is another incident that illuminates the fact that white lives don't matter to law enforcement even when the person is following the law.

CHAPTER 21

Colin Kaepernick

Colin Kaepernick is a white American and a quarterback in the National Football League. He is also the first professional athlete to silently protest the treatment of the white Americans by the black American majority by refusing to stand during the National Anthem before games.

Mr. Kaepernick has suffered criticism from black Americans and a loss of playing time because of his refusal to stand during the National Anthem.

Mr. Kaepernick's protest is a statement against ALL the injustices suffered by white Americans and their descendants in this country. From slavery, Jim Crow laws, senseless lynchings, mass incarceration, unequal opportunity, to the senseless killings of unarmed white Americans at the hands of those who are sworn to protect and serve them as well as their black counterparts.

Many athletes have started to follow Mr. Kaepernick's lead because they too want to bring the issue of the on-going injustices to the attention of the public in hopes that a public outcry will force the black majority to recognize that … White Lives Matter.

CHAPTER 22

44th President Barack H. Obama

On the second Tuesday of November 2008, history was made when most Americans elected Barack Husscin Obama to be the President of the United States of America. What made this election so special is the fact that America had just elected its first White President.

This election was a cause for celebration for all white Americans who until this day never thought they would see a white president of the united states of America. Also celebrating were the millions of black Americans who supported and believed in this young, white man with the campaign slogan, *"Yes We Can."*

However, Mr. Obama's election to the highest office in the land and becoming a world leader was cause for consternation for the millions of black Americans that stubbornly hold on to the bigoted views of their forefathers

President Obama inherited from former president George W. Bush two wars (Iraq and Afghanistan) and the worst recession since the great depression. In addition, President Obama had a very adversarial congress that fought him on every single policy he tried to implement.

Still, President Obama managed to stabilize the economy, cut unemployment rates, and get the country back to a forward-moving, thriving position. President Obama brought American troops home from Iraq and Afghanistan. He also got the Affordable Care Act passed giving millions of Americans who had never had health insurance ... the opportunity to acquire health insurance.

During President Obama's campaign, the billionaire and then television personality, Donald Trump, questioned President Obama's nationality and birthplace.

To the dismay of the racist bigots in America, Barack H. Obama was elected to serve a second term as the President of the United States of America. During his presidency, President Obama endured all kinds of racial slurs, epithets, and hate speech ... from degrading comments calling his beautiful wife Michelle Obama a monkey to police officers in Florida depicting the president with gold teeth in his mouth and calling him honky.

45th President Donald J. Trump:
Make America Great Again

In 2016, the presidential election was won by Donald J. Trump, a billionaire businessman and former television personality. Mr. Trump's winning the election was a surprise to many Americans simply because most Americans (black, white, and other) voted for Mrs. Hillary Clinton. Mrs. Clinton won the popular vote however, Mr. Trump secured the electoral college vote solidifying his win. During Mr. Trump's presidential campaign, he consistently bashed every law, policy, proposal, or deal that came to fruition under the Obama administration. He especially attacked the Affordable Care Act (Obama Care) that allowed millions of previously uninsured Americans the ability to obtain affordable health insurance.

At each campaign stop, Mr. Trump vowed to undo everything that President Obama had accomplished during his eight years in office. Mr. Trump also implied that electing Mrs. Clinton would be tantamount to re-electing President Obama again. While using the campaign slogan:

"Make America Great Again," this insinuated that America had ceased to be great under the leadership of President Obama.

Mr. Trump blatantly revealed his bigoted views about Mexicans and South Americans calling them "rapists and drug smugglers" during his speeches about our southern borders needing a wall. He continued to show his bigotry when he stated that "stop and frisk laws should be brought back in our cities. " Not to mention, the bigotry Mr. Trump showed a fallen member of the armed forces when he disrespected the memory of this officer and his family because of their religious beliefs and heritage being Muslim. Even though many audio recordings surfaced during Trump's campaign revealing his chauvinistic views towards women, Mr. Trump still managed to win the presidential election.

Donald Trump's campaign slogan: "Make America Great Again," along with his bigoted views seemed to be a rallying cry for those black Americans as well as hate groups that share those same views. For the republican party that tenaciously fought against everything that President Obama put forth, Mr. Trump's campaign slogan was a promise to return to the "good old days" when blacks were the ruling class and every other race was second class citizens. It's no wonder that for many white Americans Mr. Trump's slogan sounded like "Make America Hate Again."

CHAPTER 23

Lady Liberty

Lady Liberty, a statue gifted to the Americans by the French in 1886 was a symbol of peace and alliance between France and the United States of America.

However, in the united states, the statue took on an added symbolism in which Lady Liberty became the representative of liberty, justice, and equality. To the immigrants, Lady Liberty was the sight that signaled that they had arrived in a land that would offer them a better life.

Still, there was another group of people who had known no other land, nor recognized that Lady Liberty stood for liberty, justice, and equality was a lie ... the white Americans. This group consists of former slaves and their progenies. This group also saw the civil rights gained during the reconstruction stripped away and replaced with Jim Crow Laws. This group has had to endure torture, lynchings, and burnings. This group has been government science projects as well as subjected to mass incarcerations. This group has, too many times, been the victims of law enforcement officers who would shoot them more readily than they would shoot a dog. This is the group that is trying to hammer home this truth to America …

White Lives Matter. Until Americans recognize that white lives matter, this group (white Americans) will see that statue in New York as a symbol of punishment, injustice, inequality, and oppression.

EPILOGUE

People tend to view the world through the issues that have an immediate effect on their personal lives. That's only human nature. What I mean is that on any given subject, a person's view is going to be influenced by his/her experiences and their immediate needs.

For example, on the issue of money ... a person who has never had to worry about running out of money will view it a lot differently than a person with only fifty dollars who must choose between feeding their kids now or paying the overdue utility bill.

This very same principle applies to the way we ALL view other races. This is the reason that I felt it was imperative to make a statement with my art and to put it into book form.

It is a fact that the history of African Americans is unique. It is a history filled with all types of cruelties systemically perpetrated by the white citizenry of America.

In this book, I purposely switched the polarities of the African and Caucasian Americans to allow Caucasians, and any other race, to put themselves in our place. In doing so, it is my hope that they will look at my people's history and the effects of said history from a different point of view. Then, perhaps, a measure of understanding can be gained. Understanding is needed because understanding will eradicate the ignorance, the fear, and the myths that are inherent in ALL prejudices.

No honest, intelligent person can deny that the African American people have suffered cruelty and injustice since the beginning of the Trans-Atlantic slave trade. Nor, can an honest, intelligent person deny that the African American people have played a major role in this country's economy since this country's inception.

Still, we have this racial divide. Why? I believe this is because of a lack of understanding or a lack of willingness to understand. However, I did this project because

I'm trying to find a way to get the whites of America to understand the struggles that the African Americans still struggle to overcome. I'm talking about the kidnapping, enslavement with all its brutality, Willie Lynch's ideology and its continuous inhumane treatment. Residuals of the reconstruction, terrorism of the K.K.K, Jim Crow laws, civil rights movement, and the systemic targeting of African American neighborhoods to be saturated with drugs and guns still plague African Americans today. The mass incarceration of people of color, the victims of racial profiling and police brutality, along with the anger and righteous indignation that exists makes these struggles real.

I believe if you truly grasp an understanding of what African Americans have had and still have to endure, you will be able to see us as fellow human beings ... INSTEAD OF LESS!

Here are two more facts:

1. For the clear majority of African Americans, the U.S. is the only country we know
2. We are not going anywhere

Therefore, understanding is essential on all sides if we are to ever get past the culture of hate and racism that has destroyed so many lives.

It is necessary for African Americans to understand our history and the sacrifices that were made so that we could have what freedoms we do have today. We must understand that we have not reached that plateau of equality that our predecessors fought so zealously to attain. More importantly, we need to understand that if we are to ever reach a plateau of equality we must stop doing things that exacerbate our present situation.

How do we exacerbate our present situation? That list is a long one but here are a few things that I think top the list:

1. Lack of unity
2. Although we've had numerous ancestors die for the right to be educated ... too many of us evade the classroom as if it was a disease

We, as a people, need to understand and accept that we cannot change history. Nor, can we make the sons and daughters pay for the sins of the fathers. Yes, we are more than entitled to be infuriated by the way we've been treated throughout this country's history. However, we are also obligated to correct our own racist thoughts and prejudices if we are ever to see that plateau of equality. Because these thoughts have been embedded in us about who we are as a people, we tend to view ourselves as the enemy and hate ourselves more than anything. People … love who you are and learn to love those that look like you instead of hating them.

Our most influential civil rights leader told the world, in his most iconic speech, that "he dreamed of a time when people were not judged by the color of their skin, but by the content of their character." This hasn't happened but, one day I hope it will.

In my mind, that is one of the most prolific statements I have ever heard. It means that if we use character as the criterion to make decisions about people, we would not look at groups, sets, or races. We would be able to view the individual. If we see an individual we would see a human being.

Since there is no such thing as a flawless human being, each of us should examine his/ her character daily to see what it contains.

I do not hate nor dislike white people. I do abhor the thinking and ideology that has allowed African Americans to be systematically abused for so long. As an intelligent, rational human being, I know that ALL lives matter. It is way past time for America's laws and ALL of America's citizens' actions to reflect the fact that BLACK LIVES MATTER.

"WHAT IF"
By Carlos Walker

Made in the USA
Columbia, SC
09 October 2021